Finding True Joy

Through a Study in Psalm 119

by

Nicole Love Halbrooks Vaughn

NICOLE LOVE HALBROOKS VAUGHN

Scripture verses all from New American Standard Bible translation.

This book is a product of Proven Path Publications.

Proven Path Publications is a part of Proven Path Ministries. A ministry that exists to lead and encourage women. A ministry that strives to help women find the proven path of Christ and to persevere in their journey on it.

Author Photo made by Mandi Evans Photography

Copyright © 2016 Nicole Love Halbrooks Vaughn

All rights reserved.

ISBN:0692727272
ISBN-13:9780692727270

DEDICATION

This book is dedicated to my husband Patrick in appreciation for the time that he has allowed me to study and write this book, as well as the others that have been written, and the others that are in my heart and still to come. I love you, Patrick.

Contents

Introduction
God's Precepts in Psalm 19:7-8

Lesson One
Making God's Precepts My Own (Psalm 119:1-56)

Lesson Two
Proving God's Precepts Through Afflictions (Psalm 119:57-104)

Lesson Three
Trusting God's Precepts Through Trials and Persecutions (Psalm 119:105-144)

Lesson Four
Choosing God's Precepts No Matter The Cost (Psalm 119:145-176)

Conclusion
Closing Thoughts and Contact Information

ACKNOWLEDGMENTS

All research on Hebrew translations is from www.biblehub.com

Bible Hub Online Parallel Bible, search and study tools including parallel texts, cross references, Treasury of Scripture, and commentaries. This site provides quick access to topical studies, interlinears, sermons, Strong's and many more resources.

Their mission is best summarized as follows:
1) Increase the visibility and accessibility of the Scriptures online.

2) Provide free access to Bible study tools in many languages.

3) Promote the Gospel of Christ through the learning, study and application of God's word.

This site is a great way to link any verse on your site to an instant menu of 25 versions!

Introduction

Finding True Joy is a simple four lesson study through the longest chapter in the Bible, Psalm 119. This Psalm is one that I come to often. It focuses on the precepts of God. When I awake in the night and cannot sleep, I turn to Psalm 119. When I am struggling with present circumstances and feel the Lord is distant from me, I turn to Psalm 119. When I need to seek the face of God for direction and I am not sure where to start, I turn to Psalm 119.

What we will learn in this four lesson study is how the precepts of God do just what David said they would do in Psalm 19, rejoice the heart. The first time the word precept is used in the Bible is in Psalm 19. The Hebrew word for precept in Psalm 19:8 is *piqqud*. It is only used twenty-four times in the Scriptures. Twenty-one of those twenty-four times is in Psalm 119.

Before we start digging into what Psalm 119 teaches us about God's precepts, let's see what we can learn from looking at the Scripture passage that contains the very first use of the word. We will start with the NASB translation of Psalm 19:7-8. We are going to read it, break it down, and look at each verse individually to see what foundational truths we can learn from these verses.

All you need to complete this study is, access to a Bible (Google search will work if you do not have a Bible), and a pen to record your answers to the questions. There is plenty of blank space left on the pages of this study so that you can take notes in this book (but of course your online device could work for this as well).

After this introduction lesson you will find a passage of Psalm 119 in a box and then there will be a few question for you to ask yourself to help you dig into each passage a little deeper. I have divided the passages according to their division in the Bible. If you look up Psalm 119 in your Bible you will find it being divided by words: Aleph, Beth, Gimel, Daleth, etc. These words are simply the ABC's of the Hebrew alphabet. For me, knowing this just seems to solidify how foundational the truths of this chapter of Scripture are for us.

Let's begin.

*7 The law of the LORD is perfect, restoring the soul;
The testimony of the LORD is sure, making wise the simple.
8 The precepts of the LORD are right, rejoicing the heart;
The commandment of the LORD is pure, enlightening the eyes.*
Psalm 19:7-8

1) Use Psalm 19:7 to fill in the blanks.

The law of the LORD is _____

The Hebrew word for law in this verse is *towrat* and it means a code of law as written in the code of the covenant. It is direction, instruction, teaching, and/or law.

The Hebrew word for perfect in this verse is *tamim* and it means complete.

2) According to Psalm 19:7 what does the law of the LORD do?

_____ our soul

The Hebrew word for restoring is *shub* and it means to return, to turn back, convert, refresh

3) What's wrong with our soul? Why would it need restoring?

The Hebrew word for soul is *nephesh* and it means a soul, living being, life, self, person, desire, passion, appetite, emotion.

4) Look at the second sentence in Psalm 19:7 and fill in the blanks.

The testimony of the Lord is _____

The Hebrew word for testimony is *eduth* and it means witness. It comes from the root word uwd that means to call to, to take to record, admonish, to give warning.

5) What does the testimony of the Lord do?

_____ wise the _____

6) According to Psalm 19:7 do you have to be old and smart to understand the testimony?

_____

7) Let's look at Psalm 19:8 now and use it to answer the following the questions.

The precepts of the Lord are _____

8) What do the precepts of the Lord do?

_____ the heart

9) Let's move on to the second sentence in that verse. Look at it to fill in the blanks.

The commandment of the Lord is _____

The Hebrew word for commandment here is *mitsvah* it is in the singular, so each command is pure in and of itself.

10) What does the commandment of the Lord do?

_____ the _____

The Hebrew word for enlightens in this verse is *or* and it means to shine, to be or become light, to set on fire.

11) Look up and read Matthew 6:22-23. What do you learn about the eye in this passage?

_____

_____

_____

12) Do you see a connection between Psalm 19:7-8 and Jesus' words in Matthew 6:22-23?

_____

_____

Psalm 19:7-8 and Matthew 6:22-23 give us some hard facts straight from God. Now as we dig into Psalm 119 we are going to see how these truths are fleshed out. The words we just looked at (law, testimony, precepts, commandment, perfect, sure, right, pure, etc) will be repeated throughout Psalm 119. We will be breaking Psalm 119 down into four parts as we study this insightful chapter in the Word of God.

Before we begin any study into the Bible, we must first be willing to have an open mind and heart. We must enter every study of the Scriptures with a willingness to lay aside any preconceived notions. Are you willing to do that?

If so, let us begin with prayer…

Dear God,

I come before you now and I ask that You would open my heart and my mind to Your Word. I want to know truth and I want to know true joy. I am tired of being controlled by my emotions and my circumstances. I am seeking a solid and sure foundation on which I can stand and I am hoping that I can find that in You and in Your Word. Help me to lay aside what I have been taught and come to this study with fresh eyes. I have heard of You. I have watched those that say that they know You because of Jesus. I have seen something in them that I desire… and I am hoping that what I have seen is You. I want to know You.

Amen

Lesson One

Psalm 119:1-56

Making God's Precepts My Own

> 1 *How blessed are those whose way is blameless, who walk in the law of the LORD.*
> 2 *How blessed are those who observe His testimonies, who seek Him with all their heart.*
> 3 *They also do no unrighteousness; they walk in His ways.*
> 4 *You have ordained Your precepts, that we should keep them diligently.*
> 5 *Oh that my ways may be established to keep Your statutes!*
> 6 *Then I shall not be ashamed when I look upon all Your commandments.*
> 7 *I shall give thanks to You with uprightness of heart, when I learn Your righteous judgments.*
> 8 *I shall keep Your statutes; do not forsake me utterly!*

1. What does the writer of this Psalm observe about those who obey God's laws and testimonies in Psalm 119:1-4 and what does he observe about God's precepts?
2. How does he respond to what he has observed according to Psalm 119:5-8?

> *9 How can a young man keep his way pure? By keeping it according to Your word.*
> *10 With all my heart I have sought You; do not let me wander from Your commandments.*
> *11 Your word I have treasured in my heart, that I may not sin against You.*
> *12 Blessed are You, O LORD; teach me Your statutes.*
> *13 With my lips I have told of all the ordinances of Your mouth.*
> *14 I have rejoiced in the way of Your testimonies, as much as in all riches.*
> *15 I will meditate on Your precepts and regard Your ways.*
> *16 I shall delight in Your statutes; I shall not forget Your word.*

3. Why has he treasured God's word in his heart according to Psalm 119:9-11?
4. What does he ask God to do in Psalm 119:12?
5. What steps does the writer take in Psalm 119:13-16 to not forget God's word?

> **17** *Deal bountifully with Your servant, that I may live and keep Your word.*
> **18** *Open my eyes, that I may behold wonderful things from Your law.*
> **19** *I am a stranger in the earth; do not hide Your commandments from me.*
> **20** *My soul is crushed with longing after Your ordinances at all times.*
> **21** *You rebuke the arrogant, the cursed, who wander from Your commandments.*
> **22** *Take away reproach and contempt from me, for I observe Your testimonies.*
> **23** *Even though princes sit and talk against me, Your servant meditates on Your statutes.*
> **24** *Your testimonies also are my delight; they are my counselors*

6. What does the writer ask of God in Psalm 119:17-18?
7. Why does He ask Him to do it?
8. How does the writer refer to himself in Psalm 119:19 and Psalm 119:23?
9. What does he ask of God in Psalm 119:19-23?
10. What do you learn about God and His actions in Psalm 119:21?
11. Why does God rebuke?
12. What does the writer do with God's word in Psalm 119:20, 22-24?
13. In verse 22 the writer asks for both reproach and contempt to be taken away from him. Reproach in the Hebrew is *cherpah* and it is shame that comes from the taunt of an enemy or a circumstance in life (sexual, barrenness, hunger, uncircumcision,

injuries from enemy). Contempt in the Hebrew is *buz* and it is shame springing from pride and wickedness, springing from prosperity and ease, and shame from receiving the judgment of God. How are both of these types of shame removed or taken away?

14. What conclusion does the writer come to about the word of God in verse 24?

> **25** *My soul cleaves to the dust; revive me according to Your word.*
> **26** *I have told of my ways, and You have answered me; teach me Your statutes.*
> **27** *Make me understand the way of Your precepts, so I will meditate on Your wonders.*
> **28** *My soul weeps because of grief; strengthen me according to Your word.*
> **29** *Remove the false way from me, and graciously grant me Your law.*
> **30** *I have chosen the faithful way; I have placed Your ordinances before me.*
> **31** *I cling to Your testimonies; O LORD, do not put me to shame!*
> **32** *I shall run the way of Your commandments, for You will enlarge my heart.*

15. In Psalm 119:25-32 we see an inward struggle taking place within the soul and mind of the writer as he learns more about himself through the eyes of God as he allows God's word to counsel him. In verse 25 what does he realize his soul clings to?
16. Look up and read Genesis 3:14-19. How does this help you understand what the writer has just realized about himself?
17. In Psalm 119:31 what has the writer chosen to cling to instead and how does he ask God to help him?
18. In Psalm 119:32 what is the writer trusting the Lord to do for him?

> **33** *Teach me, O LORD, the way of Your statutes, and I shall observe it to the end.*
> **34** *Give me understanding, that I may observe Your law and keep it with all my heart.*
> **35** *Make me walk in the path of Your commandments, for I delight in it.*
> **36** *Incline my heart to Your testimonies and not to dishonest gain.*
> **37** *Turn away my eyes from looking at vanity, and revive me in Your ways.*
> **38** *Establish Your word to Your servant, as that which produces reverence for You.*
> **39** *Turn away my reproach which I dread, for Your ordinances are good.*
> **40** *Behold, I long for Your precepts; revive me through Your righteousness.*

19. What does the writer ask of God in Psalm 119:33-40?
20. How do these verses illustrate the revelation and growth that the writer has had in his walk with the Lord since the beginning of this Psalm?
21. In Psalm 119:1-3 the writer has realized some things from watching others who love God and His Word. He realizes that he wants to be like them. He realizes that it must be because they observe the law of God. However, when he chooses to try and walk like them, when he tries to live according to God's word, he realizes that he can't. By Psalm 119:17-19 he thinks he just needs more insight into God's law, more knowledge, but when he asks God to open his eyes, God lets him see the real

him. When we get to Psalm 119:27 he knows that only God can help him. He chooses to run towards God's way, but is completely dependant upon God to be able to walk in God's ways. In Psalm 119:33-40 we see a heart change in the writer which will become evident as we continue in our study of this Psalm.

22. Look up and read John 3:19-21. How does what Jesus teaches in this passage relate to the experience of the writer of Psalm 119?

> **41** *May Your lovingkindnesses also come to me, O LORD, Your salvation according to Your word;*
> **42** *So I will have an answer for him who reproaches me, for I trust in Your word.*
> **43** *And do not take the word of truth utterly out of my mouth, for I wait for Your ordinances.*
> **44** *So I will keep Your law continually, forever and ever.*
> **45** *And I will walk at liberty, for I seek Your precepts.*
> **46** *I will also speak of Your testimonies before kings and shall not be ashamed.*
> **47** *I shall delight in Your commandments, which I love.*
> **48** *And I shall lift up my hands to Your commandments, which I love; and I will meditate on Your statutes.*

23. In Psalm 119:41-44 what attitude change do you see in the writer? How does he now see those who reproach him?
24. Compare Psalm 119:45-46 with Psalm 119:21-23, how has the writer grown in his confidence in the Lord?
25. In Psalm 119:47-48 what is the writer's relationship to the commandments of God?

> **49** *Remember the word to Your servant, in which You have made me hope.*
> **50** *This is my comfort in my affliction, that Your word has revived me.*
> **51** *The arrogant utterly deride me, yet I do not turn aside from Your law.*
> **52** *I have remembered Your ordinances from of old, O LORD, and comfort myself.*
> **53** *Burning indignation has seized me because of the wicked, who forsake Your law.*
> **54** *Your statutes are my songs in the house of my pilgrimage.*
> **55** *O LORD, I remember Your name in the night, and keep Your law.*
> **56** *This has become mine, that I observe Your precepts*

26. How do we see this relationship lived out in Psalm 119:49-52?
27. What has the writer realized about himself according to Psalm 119:54?
28. Look up and read John 18:36, Romans 12:2, 2 Corinthians 5:17-20, Philippians 3:18-20, and Colossians 1:13. How do these passages relate to Psalm 119:54?
29. When does the writer remember God's name and keep His law? Compare this verse with 1 Thessalonians 5:1-11.
30. What has the writer concluded in Psalm 119:56?

Now today, as you think on all that you have learned, have you chosen God's way? Have you made God's precepts your own? The beautiful transformation that takes place within us when we take hold of God and

His truth is that of going from Romans 3:10-20 to Romans 8:1-2 to Romans 1:16-17. The whole point of the law of God was to bring us to His gospel. His gospel is found in a nutshell in 1 Corinthians 15:1-10. Look these verses up tonight and read them.

Lesson Two
Psalm 119:57-104

Proving God's Precepts Through Affliction

> **57** *The* LORD *is my portion; I have promised to keep Your words.*
> **58** *I sought Your favor with all my heart; be gracious to me according to Your word.*
> **59** *I considered my ways and turned my feet to Your testimonies.*
> **60** *I hastened and did not delay to keep Your commandments.*
> **61** *The cords of the wicked have encircled me, but I have not forgotten Your law.*
> **62** *At midnight I shall rise to give thanks to You because of Your righteous ordinances.*
> **63** *I am a companion of all those who fear You, and of those who keep Your precepts.*
> **64** *The earth is full of Your lovingkindness, O* LORD*; teach me your statutes*

1. Who is the Lord to the writer in Psalm 119:57?
2. What has the writer promised to do?
3. What has the writer done according to verse 58-60?
4. Who encircles the writer according to Psalm 119:61?
5. In verse 62 how does the writer respond when encircled by the wicked?
6. The Hebrew word for midnight in verse 62 is actually two separate words. It is broken down by the use of the word *chatsoth* which means division or middle and the Hebrew word *layil* which means midnight season. This word can mean away from the light, opposed to light, adversity, time of personal distress, etc.

7. What choices has the writer made in Psalm 119:63-64? (Hint: Who has he chosen as friends and how has he chosen to think?)

> **65** *You have dealt well with Your servant, O LORD, according to Your word.*
> **66** *Teach me good discernment and knowledge, for I believe in Your commandments.*
> **67** *Before I was afflicted I went astray, but now I keep Your word.*
> **68** *You are good and do good; teach me Your statutes.*
> **69** *The arrogant have forged a lie against me; with all my heart I will observe Your precepts.*
> **70** *Their heart is covered with fat, but I delight in Your law.*
> **71** *It is good for me that I was afflicted, that I may learn Your statutes.*
> **72** *The law of Your mouth is better to me than thousands of gold and silver pieces.*

8. In Psalm 119:65 how does the writer say the Lord has treated him and on what does he base his statement?
9. What does the writer ask of the Lord in verse 66?
10. What has the writer learned in Psalm 119:67-68?
11. Who is coming against the writer in verse in 69?
12. How has the writer chosen to respond to their attacks and lies against him?
13. Why is the writer able to respond in this way? Look at Psalm 119:70-72 and notice what the writer has learned.
14. The Hebrew word for fat in this verse is *cheleb* and it is used figurative of an unreceptive heart, their heart is as unresponsive as the midriff-fat near it. Look up and read Romans 1:21, Romans 1:32, Romans 2:5, and Romans 10:1-10. Do you believe in the LORD's commandments?

> *73 Your hands made me and fashioned me; give me understanding, that I may learn Your commandments.*
> *74 May those who fear You see me and be glad, because I wait for Your word.*
> *75 I know, O LORD, that Your judgments are righteous, and that in faithfulness You have afflicted me.*
> *76 O may Your lovingkindness comfort me, according to Your word to Your servant.*
> *77 May Your compassion come to me that I may live, for Your law is my delight.*
> *78 May the arrogant be ashamed, for they subvert me with a lie; but I shall meditate on Your precepts.*
> *79 May those who fear You turn to me, even those who know Your testimonies.*
> *80 May my heart be blameless in Your statutes, so that I will not be ashamed.*

15. In Psalm 119:73 who does the writer acknowledge God to be?
16. Why does the writer ask the Lord to give him understanding according to verses 73-74?
17. What has the writer learned about the Lord according to verses 75-76?
18. How did the writer learn these things about the Lord?
19. In Psalm 119:77-78, where has the writer learned to go when he is being lied about?
20. What kind of person has the writer decided to be according to verses 79-80

> **81** *My soul languishes for Your salvation; I wait for Your word.*
> **82** *My eyes fail with longing for Your word, while I say, "When will You comfort me?"*
> **83** *Though I have become like a wineskin in the smoke, I do not forget Your statutes.*
> **84** *How many are the days of Your servant? When will You execute judgment on those who persecute me?*
> **85** *The arrogant have dug pits for me, men who are not in accord with Your law.*
> **86** *All Your commandments are faithful; they have persecuted me with a lie; help me!*
> **87** *They almost destroyed me on earth, but as for me, I did not forsake Your precepts.*
> **88** *Revive me according to Your lovingkindness, so that I may keep the testimony of Your mouth.*

21 As we read Psalm 119:81-88 what has happened in the life of the writer?

22 Who is still attacking this servant of the Lord according to Psalm 119:85?

23 What is the writer asking the Lord to do in Psalm 119:81-86?

24 Have you ever experienced a struggle like this inside of your own heart and mind?

25 How was the Lord's servant victorious?

26 What does he ask of the Lord in Psalm 119: 88?

27 Why does the writer ask this from the Lord?

> **89** *Forever, O LORD, Your word is settled in heaven.*
> **90** *Your faithfulness continues throughout all generations; You established the earth, and it stands.*
> **91** *They stand this day according to Your ordinances, for all things are Your servants.*
> **92** *If Your law had not been my delight, then I would have perished in my affliction.*
> **93** *I will never forget Your precepts, for by them You have revived me.*
> **94** *I am Yours, save me; for I have sought Your precepts.*
> **95** *The wicked wait for me to destroy me; I shall diligently consider Your testimonies.*
> **96** *I have seen a limit to all perfection; Your commandment is exceedingly broad.*

28. Read Psalm 119:89-91, what has the writer come to know without any doubt?
29. According to Psalm 119:92-93, how has the writer made it through the tough times?
30. Compare Psalm 119:94 with Psalm 119:86, how has the writer grown in confidence as he remembered who his God is?
31. In Psalm 119:95-96 why has the writer chosen to diligently consider God's testimonies?
32. Look up and read Joshua 21:45, 1 Kings 8:56, Isaiah 40:7-8, Jeremiah 1:12, Matthew 24:35, and Luke 16:17. According to these verses whose word can be trusted?

> 97 *O how I love Your law! It is my meditation all the day.*
> 98 *Your commandments make me wiser than my enemies, for they are ever mine.*
> 99 *I have more insight than all my teachers, for Your testimonies are my meditation.*
> 100 *I understand more than the aged, because I have observed Your precepts.*
> 101 *I have restrained my feet from every evil way, that I may keep Your word.*
> 102 *I have not turned aside from Your ordinances, for You Yourself have taught me.*
> 103 *How sweet are Your words to my taste! Yes, sweeter than honey to my mouth!*
> 104 *From Your precepts I get understanding; therefore I hate every false way.*

33 What relationship does the writer now have with the law of God in Psalm 119:97?

34 The word love in the Hebrew in verse 97 is *aheb*. It is a verb and it means to love like a friend, to show love to, to have affection for. Look up and read Isaiah 41:8-9, John 15:14-15, James 2:23, and James 4:4. Now think of what you have already learned in Psalm 119:1-96, how has God proven to be a friend to the writer and how has the writer proven to be a friend of God?

35 Read Psalm 119:98-100. What has changed in the life of the reader because of his relationship with God's commandments, testimonies, and precepts?

36 Look up and read John 7:15-18 and compare it with Psalm 119:99.

37 Now look up and read Luke 21:10-15 and Colossians 1:28-2:3, how do these passages relate to what you have learned in Psalm 119?
38 What has the writer done in Psalm 119:101 so that he could keep God's word?
39 Look up and read Colossians 3:1-8. Whose responsibility is it to walk in obedience to Christ?
40 According to Psalm 119:102 why has the writer been able to stay faithful to God's ordinances?
41 Look up and read John 6:44-45, John 16:13, Romans 8:11-14, and Colossians 1:9-10. In Colossians 1:9-10 the Greek word for knowledge is *epignosis*, and it is a knowledge that comes from first hand experience. What does it mean to you to know that God Himself wants to teach you and you CAN learn first hand from Him?
42 How does the writer describe the Word of God in Psalm 119:103?
43. According to Psalm 119:104 why does the writer hate every false way? What has he learned?

In Psalm 119:1-56 the writer of this Psalm watched others who had chosen to trust in God's law and he decided that he too would choose to make God's precepts his own. Then in Psalm 119:57-104 the writer learned that choosing to walk according to God's precepts did not make him exempt from trials and hurts. He also learned that there were arrogant people out there who would afflict him just because he chose to believe and live God's way. These arrogant people could be religious, atheist, friends, family, strangers, or even our own self doubt.

In Matthew 13:1-23 Jesus tells and explains the parable of the sower. In this we see that when we hear and learn God's Word we will respond in one of four ways. The question you need to ask God is which of the four are you?

Lesson Three
Psalm 119:105-144

Trusting God's Precepts Through Trials and Persecution

> **105** *Your word is a lamp to my feet and a light to my path.*
> **106** *I have sworn and I will confirm it, that I will keep Your righteous ordinances.*
> **107** *I am exceedingly afflicted; revive me, O LORD, according to Your word.*
> **108** *O accept the freewill offerings of my mouth, O LORD, and teach me Your ordinances.*
> **109** *My life is continually in my hand, yet I do not forget Your law.*
> **110** *The wicked have laid a snare for me, yet I have not gone astray from Your precepts.*
> **111** *I have inherited Your testimonies forever, for they are the joy of my heart.*
> **112** *I have inclined my heart to perform Your statutes forever, even to the end.*

1. How does the writer describe the Word of God in Psalm 119:105?
2. What has the writer determined that he will do in Psalm 119:106?
3. How does the writer describe his affliction in Psalm 119:107?
4. The Hebrew word for exceedingly is *ad meod* and it means that until a great abundance, up to a great degree. As the writer begins to love the Word of God and His ways more do things get easier for him in this world or worse?
5. In Psalm 119:107-110, how does the writer respond to the affliction and persecution of the wicked?
6. Why does the writer respond this way?
7. What has the writer done in Psalm 119:112?

8. The word inclined in this verse is the Hebrew word *natah*. In this verse it means to bend or bow. It is used as an infinitive in this verse. An infinitive is a word that is based on a verb and therefore expresses action or a state of being. The subject in this verse is the heart.
9. Look up and read 2 Chronicles 32:26, Isaiah 66:2, Matthew 11:29, Philippians 2:8, 1 Peter 5:6-7, and Romans 6:17. Whose responsibility is it to humble the heart?

> 113 *I hate those who are double-minded, but I love Your law.*
> 114 *You are my hiding place and my shield; I wait for Your word.*
> 115 *Depart from me, evildoers, that I may observe the commandments of my God.*
> 116 *Sustain me according to Your word, that I may live; and do not let me be ashamed of my hope.*
> 117 *Uphold me that I may be safe, that I may have regard for Your statutes continually.*
> 118 *You have rejected all those who wander from Your statutes, for their deceitfulness is useless.*
> 119 *You have removed all the wicked of the earth like dross; therefore I love Your testimonies.*
> 120 *My flesh trembles for fear of You, and I am afraid of Your judgments.*

10. Who does the writer say that he hates in Psalm 119:113?
11. The Hebrew word for double-minded in verse 113 is *seeph* and it means divided, half-hearted, skeptic.
12. Look up and read James 1:2-8, how does this compare to Psalm 119:113-114?
13. In Psalm 119:115-120 who has the writer chosen to fear and who has the writer chosen to separate from?

> 121 *I have done justice and righteousness; do not leave me to my oppressors.*
> 122 *Be surety for Your servant for good; do not let the arrogant oppress me.*
> 123 *My eyes fail with longing for Your salvation and for Your righteous word.*
> 124 *Deal with Your servant according to Your lovingkindness and teach me Your statutes.*
> 125 *I am Your servant; give me understanding, that I may know Your testimonies.*
> 126 *It is time for the LORD to act, for they have broken Your law.*
> 127 *Therefore I love Your commandments above gold, yes, above fine gold.*
> 128 *Therefore I esteem right all Your precepts concerning everything, I hate every false way.*

14. In Psalm 119:121 what has the writer done? How has he lived?
15. In Psalm 119:122 what does he ask the Lord to be for him?
16. How has the writer's attitude changed as he talks about those who oppress him? (Look back at Psalm 119:84.)
17. How hard has the writer been seeking after God in His Word according to verse 123?
18. Read Psalm 119:124, whose love is the writer depending on? His for God or God's for him?
19. In Psalm 119:124, the phrase lovingkindness can also be translated as *Your covenant loyalty*. With this in mind look up and read Deuteronomy 7:9 and Daniel 9:4. If God was this faithful before the cross, how much more so after? The cross of

Christ allows us to have His Holy Spirit inside of us as a pledge of assurance (2 Corinthians 1:22, 2 Corinthians 5:5, Ephesians 1:14)!

20. According to Psalm 119:125-128 has the writer ever discovered a time when God's precepts were not valuable or right?

> **129** *Your testimonies are wonderful; therefore my soul observes them.*
> **130** *The unfolding of Your words gives light; it gives understanding to the simple.*
> **131** *I opened my mouth wide and panted, for I longed for Your commandments.*
> **132** *Turn to me and be gracious to me, after Your manner with those who love Your name.*
> **133** *Establish my footsteps in Your word, and do not let any iniquity have dominion over me.*
> **134** *Redeem me from the oppression of man, that I may keep Your precepts.*
> **135** *Make Your face shine upon Your servant, and teach me Your statutes.*
> **136** *My eyes shed streams of water, because they do not keep Your law.*

21. What did the writer observed about the Lord's testimonies in Psalm 119:129?

22. In Matthew 22:36-40 Jesus is asked what is the greatest commandment. The answer is to love the Lord your God with all your heart, all your mind, and all your soul. In Psalm 119:10-11 we see the writer choose to treasure the word of God with his heart. In Psalm 119:97 we see the writer choose to love the law of God with his mind. Now in Psalm 119:129 we see that the writer observes the testimonies of God in his soul.

23. In Psalm 119:130-131, what process do you see that the writer has gone through in order to gain this understanding and love for God and His word?

24. In Psalm 119:132-133, who has the writer realized he is completely dependant upon in order to keep the Word of God and not sin against Him?
25. Why does the writer ask the Lord to redeem him from the oppression of man?
26. Look up and read Daniel 3:16-18, Isaiah 2:22, Isaiah 51:7, Matthew 10:28, 1 Peter 3:14, and Revelation 2:10. What is the command to us in each of these verses?
27. In Psalm 119:135-136 how has the writer's attitude changed towards those who oppress him?

> **137** *Righteous are You, O LORD, and upright are Your judgments.*
> **138** *You have commanded Your testimonies in righteousness and exceeding faithfulness.*
> **139** *My zeal has consumed me, because my adversaries have forgotten Your words.*
> **140** *Your word is very pure, therefore Your servant loves it.*
> **141** *I am small and despised, yet I do not forget Your precepts.*
> **142** *Your righteousness is an everlasting righteousness, and Your law is truth.*
> **143** *Trouble and anguish have come upon me, yet Your commandments are my delight.*
> **144** *Your testimonies are righteous forever; give me understanding that I may live.*

28. In Psalm 119:137-139 what has the writer come to know about the Lord? What has he come to know about his adversaries?
29. In Psalm 119:140 why does this servant of God love the Word?
30. In Psalm 119:141 what has the writer learned about himself?
31. In Psalm 119:142-144 what has the writer learned about God's righteousness?
32. Look up and read Romans 10:1-13. How does this relate to what you have learned from the writer's experience in Psalm 119?

Through persecution the writer of this Psalm learned that those who persecuted him did so because they did not know God. They did not observe the Word of God in their heart and in their mind and in their soul. They had forgotten God and who He was and is. They might be those who knew God's word, but God's word was not their delight. They did not love God more than the approval of men. They did not love Him more than their own selves and this was why they were persecuting. However, the writer had chosen to trust his righteousness to God, his life to God, his future to God. He chose to believe God. The question today is… will you?

Lesson Four

Psalm 119:145-176

Choosing God's Precepts No Matter The Cost

> **145** *I cried with all my heart; answer me, O LORD! I will observe Your statutes.*
> **146** *I cried to You; save me and I shall keep Your testimonies.*
> **147** *I rise before dawn and cry for help; I wait for Your words.*
> **148** *My eyes anticipate the night watches, that I may meditate on Your word.*
> **149** *Hear my voice according to Your lovingkindness; revive me, O LORD, according to Your ordinances.*
> **150** *Those who follow after wickedness draw near; they are far from Your law.*
> **151** *You are near, O LORD, and all Your commandments are truth.*
> **152** *Of old I have known from Your testimonies that You have founded them forever.*

1. What is still going on in the life of the writer in Psalm 119:145-150?
2. Why is he still being persecuted according to Psalm 119:150?
3. Who does the writer know is near even though he is being hurt by those who are far away from the law of God?
4. How long has the Lord's testimonies been founded and how long will they stand?

> **153** *Look upon my affliction and rescue me, for I do not forget Your law.*
> **154** *Plead my cause and redeem me; revive me according to Your word.*
> **155** *Salvation is far from the wicked, for they do not seek Your statutes.*
> **156** *Great are Your mercies, O LORD; revive me according to Your ordinances.*
> **157** *Many are my persecutors and my adversaries, yet I do not turn aside from Your testimonies.*
> **158** *I behold the treacherous and loathe them, because they do not keep Your word.*
> **159** *Consider how I love Your precepts; revive me, O LORD, according to Your lovingkindness.*
> **160** *The sum of Your word is truth, and every one of Your righteous ordinances is everlasting.*

5. Read Psalm 119:153-159, what phrase do you see repeated three times? Look back at Psalm 119:124 and Psalm 119:149.
6. What and Who is the writer trusting in no matter what?
7. Remember the Hebrew word for lovingkindness in Psalm 119:159 can also be translated "Your covenant loyalty." A covenant is not just a contract. It is a solemn binding agreement that is greater than a conditional contract. It is to be unconditional kept. If a covenant is broken, then the consequences of that break will be unconditionally dealt out. However, God is not a man. He never breaks His covenant. In Genesis 3:15 God made a covenant with us that He would redeem us. All we have to do is trust in Him. From

Genesis 3, to the cross, to the present day, God has kept this covenant. Not one single word, not one single promise, that He has made to us has failed.

8. What conclusion has the writer come to in Psalm 119:160?

> **161** *Princes persecute me without cause, but my heart stands in awe of Your words.*
> **162** *I rejoice at Your word, as one who finds great spoil.*
> **163** *I hate and despise falsehood, but I love Your law.*
> **164** *Seven times a day I praise You, because of Your righteous ordinances.*
> **165** *Those who love Your law have great peace, and nothing causes them to stumble.*
> **166** *I hope for Your salvation, O LORD, and do Your commandments.*
> **167** *My soul keeps Your testimonies, and I love them exceedingly.*
> **168** *I keep Your precepts and Your testimonies, for all my ways are before You.*

9. Who is persecuting the writer in Psalm 119:161? Does this relate today?
10. How does the writer respond to this persecution according to Psalm 119:161-164?
11. In Psalm 119:165 what do those who love the law of God have and what is the result of having it?
12. What is the writer hoping for in Psalm 119:166? What is he doing while he hopes?
13. Look up and read Romans 5:1-5, Romans 8:23-25, Hebrews 11:1-2, James 1:22-25, and James 2:14-23. How does these verses relate to Psalm 119:166?
14. Read Psalm 119:167-168, how does the writer prove that he loves the Word of God?
15. Look up and read John 14:15, 21, 23. How did Jesus say that we prove that we love Him?

> **169** *Let my cry come before You, O LORD; give me understanding according to Your word.*
> **170** *Let my supplication come before You; deliver me according to Your word.*
> **171** *Let my lips utter praise, for You teach me Your statutes.*
> **172** *Let my tongue sing of Your word, for all Your commandments are righteousness.*
> **173** *Let Your hand be ready to help me, for I have chosen Your precepts.*
> **174** *I long for Your salvation, O LORD, and Your law is my delight.*
> **175** *Let my soul live that it may praise You, and let Your ordinances help me.*
> **176** *I have gone astray like a lost sheep; seek Your servant, for I do not forget Your commandments.*

16. What repeated phrase do you see again in Psalm 119:169-170?
17. Why will the writer's lips utter praise in Psalm 119:171?
18. What will his tongue do in Psalm 119:172?
19. Look up and read Luke 6:45, Ephesians 5:15-20, and Colossians 3:15-17. What comes forth from your tongue and what does that say about the condition of your heart?
20. In Psalm 119:173-175 what has the writer chosen?
21. Who does the writer ask to help him keep the precepts of God?
22. What does the writer ask of the Lord in Psalm 119:176?

23. Look up and read Luke 15:3-7, John 10:11-16, and 1 Peter 2:25. How do these verses help you understand what the writer asks of God?

God is mindful that we are but sheep who desperately need a Shepherd. He knows that as we seek to live for Him in this life there will be times that we are prone to wander. There will be times that persecutions, trials, and tribulation might make us doubt His love for us, but we love Him because He first loved us. When we choose His precepts no matter the cost, it is only because He first chose us (John 15:16).

In Romans 3:19-24 we learn what the writer of Psalm 119 learned. We learn that the law of God proves that we are sinners. None of us can keep His commands perfectly all the time. We all have fallen short. In Romans 5:6-8 we learn that while we were helpless sinners, actually dead in our sin (Ephesians 2:1), Christ died for us. He came for us when we could do nothing for Him or for ourselves. He came for us simply because He promised us that He would and He always keeps His promises.

If He came for us when we were dead in our sin, will He not even more come for us when we have believed in Him and chosen Him in return? Today, the question is are you His? Have you chosen His precepts? Will you chose to love Him and to obey Him no matter the cost?

Conclusion

You have completed your study in Psalm 119. I have kept this study simple with little commentary because I wanted you to be alone with God and His Word. I pray that as you complete this study you will allow God's precepts to resonate in your heart. I pray that what David learned, what the writer of this Psalm learned, and what I myself have learned will also be learned by you. God's precepts are indeed right and they most certainly do rejoice the heart.

True joy can be found.

In John 15:10-11, Jesus said "If you keep My commandments, you will abide in My love; just as I have kept My Father's commandments and abide in His love. These things I have spoken to you so that My joy may be in you, and *that* your joy may be made full."

True joy is found in and through obedience to our Creator God. He created us for Him and in His image. He came in the person of Jesus Christ so that His relationship to us and our image in Him could be restored. We will never have joy or peace apart from Him because without Him we will always be searching, never at rest, never satisfied.

Beloved, might Your mind find rest. May your soul be restored. May His joy be in you, and may your joy be made full.

Blessings in Christ,
Nicole Love Halbrooks Vaughn

You can follow Nicole's writing and teaching at Proven Path Ministries:

www.provenpathministries.com

ABOUT THE AUTHOR

Nicole Love Halbrooks Vaughn is the founder of Proven Path Ministries. She has been married to Patrick Vaughn for seventeen years. They have three beautiful girls together. Nicole is a trained Precept Ministries Bible Study Leader. She has been leading Precept studies since 2004. She is a speaker and writer and faithfully serves with her family at their home church, Central Baptist, in Decatur, AL.